FRANK SLIDE

J. William Kerr Ph.D., P. Geol.

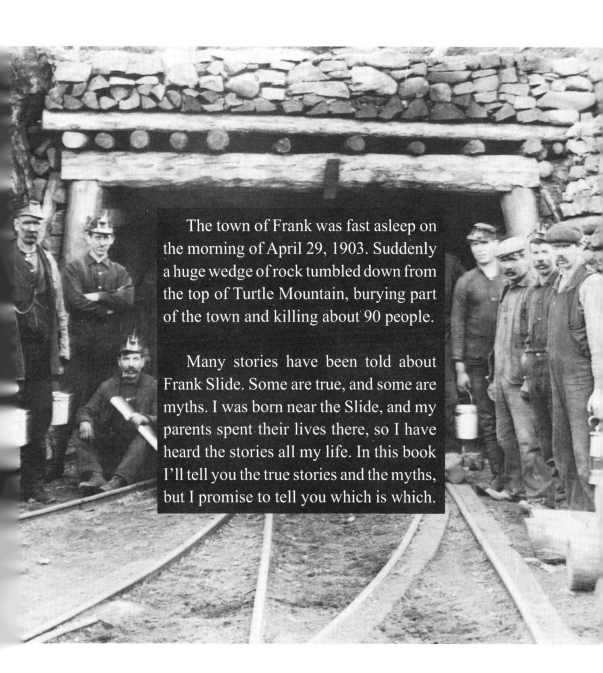

The town of Frank was fast asleep on the morning of April 29, 1903. Suddenly a huge wedge of rock tumbled down from the top of Turtle Mountain, burying part of the town and killing about 90 people.

Many stories have been told about Frank Slide. Some are true, and some are myths. I was born near the Slide, and my parents spent their lives there, so I have heard the stories all my life. In this book I'll tell you the true stories and the myths, but I promise to tell you which is which.

Before the Slide

The Town of Frank before the Slide, looking along Dominion Avenue.

In April, 1903, Frank was a coal mining boom town. It was only two years old, but had grown quickly to a population of about 600, largely because of the imagination and drive of two colourful promoters. Sam Gebo had acquired an excellent coal seam in the Crowsnest Pass in 1901, with the financial backing of Henry Frank, an entrepreneur from Butte, Montana. Together the two men formed the Canadian American Coal and Coke Company, opened a mine and built up a town beside it.

Mr. Frank saw fit to name the town after himself. Gebo became manager of the mine, but also was overseer of the townsite, chairman of the school trustees, and postmaster. The Province of Alberta did not come into being until 1905, so Frank was within the Northwest Territories for the first few years of its life.

Henry Frank, founder of the town.

Frank and Gebo put on a grand celebration to inaugurate the town on Sept. 10, 1901, and special trains from Cranbrook and Lethbridge brought the guests. Among them were Sir Frederick Haultain, Premier of the Northwest Territories, and his Minister of Public Works, Hon. A.L. Sifton, who later became Premier of Alberta. Everything was free for the residents and visitors on that special day. There were sporting events, dining, dancing, and speeches. Two thousand pounds of fresh fruit and ice cream was brought in from Spokane, and more than 900 people sat down to a lavish dinner in the open. With such a beginning, it was said that Frank would be a metropolis to rival Pittsburg.

The coal seam at Frank was large, rich, and fairly easy to mine, so the town prospered. By 1903 it had a bank, post office, hotels, stores, a town hall, and other amenities. The weekly newspaper, the Frank Sentinel, advertised a man's suit for $11.00, and two tins of salmon for 25 cents. At the time of the Slide, in April, 1903, Gebo was in Montreal, looking for investors, and promoting Frank as 'the world's richest coal mine.' But then disaster struck.

Turtle Mountain before the Slide.

Turtle Mountain before the Slide, showing the part of the mountain that fell, and at left the seven houses on Manitoba Avenue that were destroyed.

The top of Turtle Mountain was very hard limestone that did not erode easily. The base was very soft, being shale with some sandstone and a coal seam. Over millions of years the soft base of the mountain was eroded away by the river, while the limestone at the top remained and became a ledge. As erosion continued, the support at the base was removed and the limestone face became steeper. It was an unstable situation, waiting for some event to trigger a landslide.

Turtle Mountain was just south of the Town of Frank and loomed over it. The mountain was magnificent, but was also a drawback because it put Frank in the shade very early in the day. This was a minor problem in the summer, when the sun is high. But in winter the sun is low, and on Christmas day it would set at about 1:30 p.m. Early darkness was a small price to pay for living in a town with such a rosy future.

There is an interesting legend about Turtle Mountain and the native Indians. According to this legend, the Indians refused to camp where Frank was located because they thought the mountain would tumble down upon them. They called it 'The Mountain That Moves' because there were cracks on the back side and pieces fell off the front. Because it moved slowly and had a turtle shape, they called it 'Turtle Mountain,' and early settlers picked up the name.

The climax of the legend was that the night before the Slide the Indian Chief visited the Mayor of Frank and tried to convince him to move the people away because the mountain was about to fall. The advice was ignored.

There is a bit of truth to the legend. The Indians apparently did call it 'The Mountain That Moves,' would not camp beside it, and had told the white man of their concern. But there the truth ends. The name Turtle was actually given to the mountain by a rancher from Pincher Creek, because it had the shape of a turtle, including a projecting head. And the story of the late night visit to the mayor was just a yarn.

The Slide at Frank, N.W.T.

At 4:10 a.m. on April 29, 1903, a huge mass of limestone broke loose from the top of Turtle Mountain. It slid down the mountain, breaking into fragments that ranged in size from tiny chips to chunks the size of a house. The rock ploughed through the bed of the Crowsnest River, carrying both water and underlying sediments along with it, crossed the valley and hurled itself up the opposite slope to a height of 400 feet. The Slide probably lasted less than a hundred seconds but it buried everything in its path.

One of seven houses on Manitoba Avenue that was in the path of the Slide. The Bansemer family was asleep in this house and all survived unhurt. Some of the other houses were completely buried and the occupants were all killed.

Eyewitness accounts of the Slide

A train in the mine yard was backing up to the tipple* to attach a coal car, when the engineer heard rocks breaking away from the mountain above him. He quickly changed to full speed ahead and drove out of danger. The trainmen saw the men at the tipple become alarmed and start to run, but they were overtaken by the Slide and perished. Immediately afterward, everything was shrouded in a cloud of dust.

Mr. McLean kept a boarding house in Frank, and was already awake. He saw the rocks rush by only a few feet from his door and thought there had been an eruption.

Miss Higginbotham took this photo of Frank six hours after the Slide. She stood on the slide rock near Manitoba Avenue, facing west toward the town.

*Tipple - a building where waste rock is removed from the coal and the coal is then loaded onto railway cars.

View from the top of Turtle Mountain in 1911, showing how the slide rock spread out like a giant hand. An arrow shows the largest rock in the Slide.

Karl Cornelianson lived about a quarter of a mile from the edge of the Slide, and was awakened by the noise. He rushed to the door and looked toward the mine, thinking there had been an explosion. Seeing nothing there, he looked to his left and saw rock hurling itself upward on the north side of the valley, and then with its momentum spent, fall back to a lower level.

Jim Warrington, was wakened by the noise and thought it was hail. He jumped out of bed, and the next thing he knew he was forty feet from where the house had stood. His bed was some twenty feet farther on. His thigh was broken and small fragments of debris were forced into his body. He had pulled himself out of the rocks, and was working his way to some crying children when rescuers arrived.

Young Lester Johnson slept through the Slide, and woke to find himself under the floor of the house. He escaped through a small hole between the floor and the surface of the rocks. Lester was seriously injured by a splinter that pierced his abdomen, but was able to walk to safety. When the splinter was removed some feathers came with it, having come from his feather quilt. His mother and step-brother were both killed.

Many who were wakened by the Slide said that there was a distinct thud as the rocks struck the valley bottom, but the shock differed entirely from an earthquake. They also described a noise that was similar to the sound of steam escaping under high pressure, and they remarked on the terrific wind that accompanied the Slide.

Was the entire town covered, with a bank full of cash?

It is widely thought that the entire town of Frank was covered by the Slide, including the Union Bank of Canada. Stories abound that the bank had $25,000, $125,000, or $500,000 in U.S. silver dollars, or gold bullion, ready for pay day. The manager, Mr. Farmer, was said to live above the bank (he didn't), and keep four loaded pistols to protect the money.

There have been many plans to retrieve the money, with great speculation about who would own it, and whether it would have to be shared with the bank. Most of the kids in the Pass, including the author, considered looking for it at one time or another.

Well, fortunately, or unfortunately, depending on how you look at it, the rocks missed the bank completely. In a photo of Dominion Avenue taken the morning after the Slide and shown here, the undisturbed building can be seen, with a sign on it saying 'BANK.'

Enlargement of part of the photo on page 17, showing the bank.

The idea that the bank was buried was just wishful thinking, but the wishes extended to exaggerating the amount of money it contained. A miner made about $22.00 a week, so even the low figure of $25,000.00 was a week's wages for more than 1,100 miners, many times more than were ever on the payroll.

9

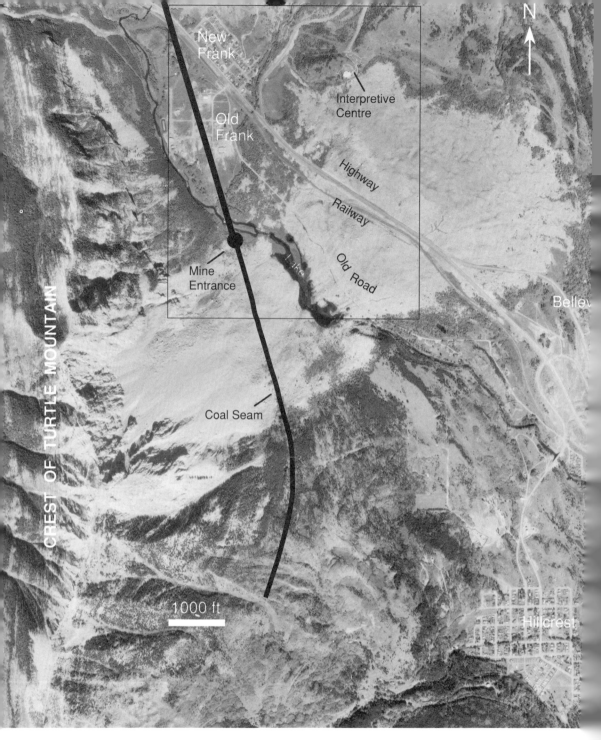

Air-photo of the Slide in 1988. The rock broke away from the crest of Turtle Mountain, slid down over the coal seam and mine entrance, and crossed the river, road and railway. Most of the construction shown here was built after the Slide. Alberta Forestry, Lands and Wildlife photograph.

Map of the Slide Area in 1903

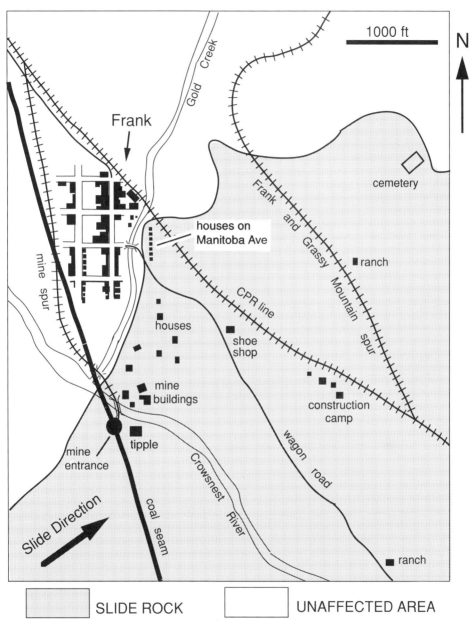

1000 ft

N

Frank

Gold Creek

Frank and Grassy Mountain spur

cemetery

houses on Manitoba Ave

ranch

mine spur

CPR line

houses

shoe shop

mine buildings

construction camp

tipple

mine entrance

wagon road

Crowsnest River

Slide Direction

coal seam

ranch

SLIDE ROCK		UNAFFECTED AREA

The Slide covered only a mall part of the main town, the row of seven houses on Manitoba Avenue. East of town it buried some outlying houses, two ranches, and a construction camp, as well as the mine entrance, and nearby mine buildings. The Slide missed the central part of town where most of the people lived. The location of this map is shown on page 10.

The miners trapped underground

Twenty men were working night shift at the mine when the Slide occurred. Seventeen were underground and they all escaped. Two had been underground, but had brought loads of coal out of the mine to the tipple, and stayed to eat their 4:00 a.m. lunch with the weighman. All three perished.

The night shift was a small crew that began work at midnight. The men worked alone or in pairs and were widely scattered throughout the mine. They maintained the equipment and tunnels for the large day shift that would follow and do most of the mining.

The coal seam was shaped like a wall extending from north to south (pages 10 and 11). It was horizontal when formed, but became tipped up to a near vertical position millions of years ago when the mountains were created. If you hold this book open with both hands, and face west with the top tilted slightly toward you, the diagram below will have the same orientation as the mine does. The book will represent the coal seam, a wall averaging 14 feet thick, trending north, and dipping to the west at five degrees from the vertical.

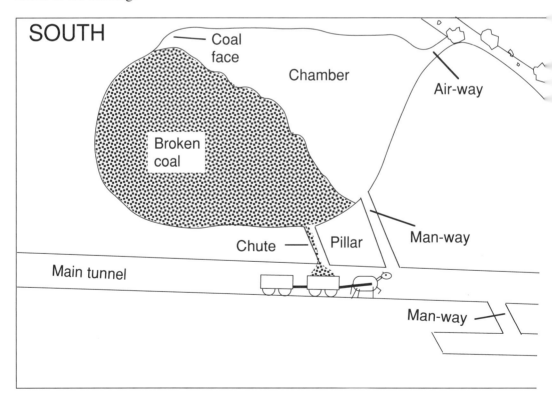

SOUTH

Coal face

Chamber

Air-way

Broken coal

Man-way

Chute — Pillar

Man-way

Main tunnel

All of the mining activity took place within the coal seam, and the miners tried to remove as much of the coal as they could. First they drove th emain tunnel along the seam for about a mile, and propped it up with timbers to prevent its collapse. Then they dug narrow chutes and man-ways upward through the coal, leaving large pillars between them to prevent the side walls from collapsing, Above that, they mined coal with picks and shovels, breaking it off the walls and roof of large chambers that were up to 400 feet high, 150 feet wide, and as thick as the seam. The broken coal was stored in the chambers until it was needed, and then was pushed down chutes into coal cars waiting below on railway tracks in the main tunnel.

The Frank Mine was inside the low hills that are the eastern foot of Turtle Mountain. The mine entrance was near the river, and the main tunnel extended southward from it within the seam.

The slide rock came down from the crest of Turtle Mountain, and travelled northeast (page 10). As it passed over the mine it filled in the entrance, and its weight caused nearby parts of the tunnel to collapse.

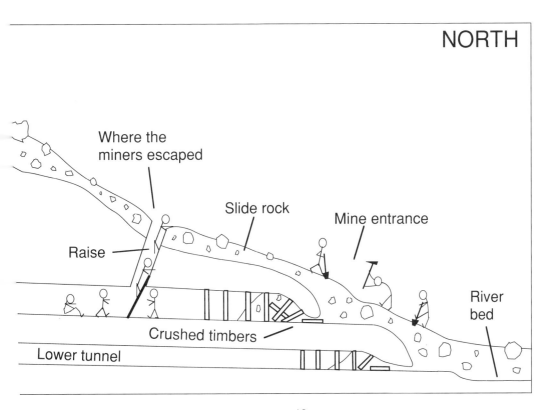

NORTH

Where the miners escaped

Slide rock

Mine entrance

Raise

River bed

Crushed timbers

Lower tunnel

The miners discover they are trapped

When the Slide occurred, everyone in the mine felt a tremendous shaking and a blast of air that blew out their lights. Men and horses were thrown off their feet. They were not sure what the shaking was, but they knew what to do. Their automatic reaction was to rush to the mine entrance and get above ground to safety.

Joe Chapman, the forman , was working in a man-way about a mile from the entrance. He became aware that something was wrong when coal began to break loose, and he noted that it was 4:00 a.m. Becoming alarmed, he began to climb down a ladder to the main tunnel, when suddenly a blast of air slammed him against the wall. Recovering, he raced along the tracks toward the entrance.

Dan McKenzie,was working in a raise about three quarters of a mile from the entry. The rush of wind and a shower of falling rock flung him against the wall, cutting his head. Ignoring the wound, he rushed down to the main tunnel and ran along it toward the entrance.

Alex Grant and his partner were checking trackage when they felt the shock. They thought it was a gas explosion, and instinctively headed for the entrance. As they followed the tunnel it heaved and twisted, and they were showered by falling coal.

William Warrington was caught by collapsing rock. His friends helped dig him out before he was smothered, and he too, made it to the entrance.

Upon reaching the entrance, the miners found it blocked by a mass of fallen rock and broken timbers. Gradually, all seventeen men arrived there, breathless from their frantic dashes for safety. After a short rest they considered what to do. One option was to dig their way through the rubble to the outside. Being familiar with the track and tunnel, they tried to work out how far they would need to dig. Their estimates of the distance ranged from 50 to 300 feet. It was in fact 130 feet.

The miners dig their way out of the mine

Before digging, the miners explored the lower tunnel, which was used for air supply, hoping its entrance was open. They were shocked to find that it was rapidly filling with water. It was seeping in from the rising river that had been dammed by the Slide.

Then a party of three went back 4,000 feet into the mine by the main tunnel, and climbed into a chamber to see if they could escape through an air-way. They found that the air-ways were blocked, but also that lethal coal gas was accumulating at high levels.

Now they knew the dangers they faced. They were sealed in by rising water and the blocked entrance, and they were quickly consuming their air supply while it also was being fouled by gas.

They then decided to dig their way to the entrance, through the broken rock and crushed timbers. They worked hard but made little progress, and some of them began to panic. Then one took charge, it is unclear now who he was. He remembered that the coal seam outcropped on the mountain some distance back from the entrance. If they were close enough to the surface they could dig a raise upward through the seam and escape. It might be too far, and there might be impossible obstacles, but it was worth a try. Starting at about 7:00 a.m., they worked in relays of two or three at a time, slowly advancing.

As the afternoon dragged on, their oxygen supply diminished. Earlier they had sung to sustain their courage, but now they were quiet, conserving their last bit of air and energy. At about 5:00 p.m., while the others slumped from exhaustion, three of them struggled on. Suddenly, McKenzie's pick broke into the open and he found the wonderful air and sunlight they sought. They were free. They had been trapped for 13 hours, and had dug their way to freedom through 20 feet of coal and nine feet of limestone boulders.

The mine entrance covered by slide rock.
X - *where the trapped miners dug their way out to the surface.*
XX - *the mine entrance, where the rescue party dug into the slide rock in an attempt to find the miners.*

The miners return to the town

McKenzie was the first man out of the mine and was awed by the scene of destruction below. The Slide fanned out from the base of the mountain like a giant hand. Fifty yards below him was a small group of men digging away where the mine entrance had been. It was a rescue party that had just found the entrance and was starting to dig.

There was tremendous excitement and exchange of news when the two groups met. They had a mixture of joy and sadness as each miner learned whether his loved ones were alive or dead. Then the miners were escorted to town where they were met with a great welcome.

Main street of Frank a few hours after the Slide. Compare with page 2. The miners had just escaped, and were being escorted to town. The wagon is carrying the injured miner, William Warrington, to hospital. The scar that the Slide left on Turtle Mountain is in the background. Part of this photograph is enlarged on page 9 and shows the bank, untouched by the Slide.

Barroom of the Imperial Hotel in Frank, after the Slide.

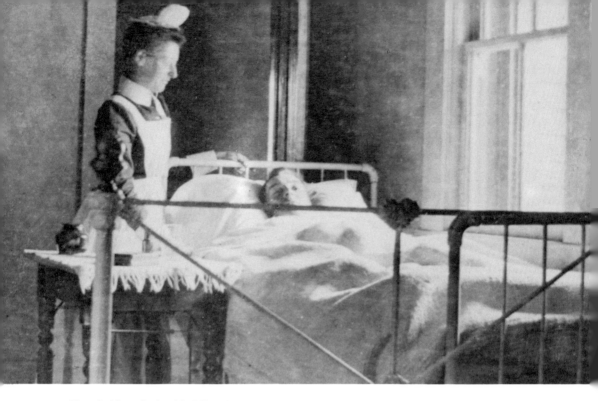

Frank Hospital with Miss Moodie and a patient. No one who escaped alive from the Slide died as a direct result of his injuries.

Post of the North West Mounted Police (NWMP) at Frank, a few days after the Slide. Reinforcements were brought in to assist in the rescue operations. Two nurses are at the doorway of the Post.

Charlie - the horse that almost made it.

When the mine was re-opened thirty one days after the Slide, Charlie, one of three horses trapped there, was still alive. He survived by drinking water that seeped in, and by gnawing the mine timbers. But he was unable to survive the welcome of his rescuers. A well meaning workman gave him a big feed of grain. It was too strong a meal after so long a fast, and he died within a few hours.

If Charlie had lived, he might have gone back to his old job. The horses were used to haul loaded coal cars out of the mine on a small railway.

How many people were killed by Frank Slide?

The exact number is not known. These estimates have been given over the years: however the figure of 90 dead is probably the most accurate.

56	Winnipeg Free Press, Apr. 30, 1903
60 to 80	Cranbrook Herald, Apr. 30, 1903
63	Report of Supt. Primrose, NWMP, 1904
66	Sign beside the highway in the Slide for years
70	Frank Sentinel Newspaper, May 2, 1903
70	Geological Survey of Canada, 1904, 1912
76	Toronto Sunday Star, Apr. 17, 1983
76	Elk Valley, Crowsnest Advertiser, Oct. 28, 1985
76	The Frank Slide Story, Anderson, 1979
80	Canadian Mining Review, 1903
100	Canadian Engineer, 1903

The Frank Sentinel Newspaper gave this list

DEAD

Alex Leitch, wife and four boys
Charles Ackroyd, wife, and one child
J. Graham, wife and two grown up sons
A. Graham and wife
J. Van Dusen, wife and two children

G. Williams, wife and three children
A. Clark, wife and six children
Mrs. W. Warrington and seven children
Two halfbreeds named Johnson
Six unknown men

J. Siotta	A. Dawes	J. W. Clark
A. Grissick Jr.	R. J. Watt	T. R. Locke
B. Cumus	F. Rochett	E. Krusa
F. Vocken	T. Delap	J. Gustavus
J. McVeigh	A. Tashgian	G. Lemosike
J. J. Scott	— Madigan	D. Yonack
Joe Britton	T. Foster	
F. Farrington	A. Dixon	

J. Warrington, fractured thigh	A. Watkins, shock
L. Ackroyd, splinter penetrating liver	S. Ennis, wife and four children
Mrs. Watkins, internal injuries	W. Warrington, leg hurt
	D. McKenzie, chest hurt

Was Frankie Slide the only survivor?

The most appealing and enduring myth associated with Frank Slide is the story of Frankie Slide. A baby of 18 months lived in one of the houses that was destroyed, but she was unharmed.

No one is quite sure who found her, how she was saved, or where she was found, but there are plenty of stories. They say she was found on a rock, on a bale of hay, in her crib, in an attic, on a pile of debris, under the roof of the house, as well as in her dead mother's arms.

It was said that the baby was the only survivor of the Slide, and that the local people did not know her name, so they called her Frankie Slide. The story was told and retold so many times it became a legend and a song was written about her. The truth is that the neighbours knew she was Marion Leitch. Her parents and her four brothers did indeed perish in their home, probably never waking from their sleep. There were other survivors, however, including her two older sisters, who were sleeping in the same house.

Luckily, Marion was found. She was raised by an uncle and aunt in Cranbrook, B.C, and married Lawrence McPhail. They lived in Nelson, and Victoria, B.C., where she died in 1977. Marion was a school teacher and also gave music lessons. The McPhails had a daughter Sheila, and two grandchildren.

Who were the other survivors?

All of those who were in Frank during the Slide, and lived to tell about it, were survivors in a sense, and they number more than 500. But the real survivors were those who were in the path of the Slide and came out alive.

The 17 coal miners were real survivors, and were saved because they were underground. There were 23 others, mostly children, who were in the path of the Slide and lived through it. They survived because they were in houses near the edge of the area covered, where the slide rock was thin.

The Ennis family was lucky. Sam was pinned under the timbers of his home, but managed to free himself, his wife and three of his four children. Baby Gladys, 15 months old, was found in a pile of mud and was believed dead. Her mother wrapped he rin a blanket and took her to a neighbor's. To everyone's surprise she was alive and unhurt. Sam's feet were cut from walking on the rocks, his wife had a broken collarbone, and the children were scratched and bruised, but all survived.

The Ennis family after they survived the Slide. When their home was destroyed they moved to Blairmore and lived in a tent. From left to right are Mrs. Ennis, Delbert, Arthur, Sam with baby Gladys, Hazel, and Jim Warrington (Mrs. Ennis' brother).

Mrs. Ennis refused to live in Frank again so the family moved to nearby Blairmore. Sam was stable boss in Frank and kept his job there. Gladys and her mother often drove the horse and buggy to pick him up after work.

Gladys Ennis grew up and married Emile Verquin. In 1990 she was 88 and they were living near Seattle. She said that reporters thought *she* was Frankie Slide, and pestered her so much that she hid the story from her children.

The story of Frankie Slide may continue to improve with time, and in another generation or two it may take on even more colour. It is amusing that not only did Frankie Slide not exist, but now there appear to have been two of them, Marion Leitch and Gladys Ennis.

Gladys Ennis Verquin on the right with three younger generations of her family. From the left are her daughter Marion Cathcart, granddaughter Arlene Olson, and her great granddaughter, Hayley Olson.

Gladys found that she did more talking about the Frank Slide after she moved from the Pass than in all the years she had lived there. "Living there, we never talked about the Slide any more. It was just there. It was something terrible that had happened in our lives, but that was in the past."

Coincidences: alive or dead by a quirk of fate

There were many cases of people who were in Frank by accident and were killed, and others who were absent by accident and were saved. A few cases are described.

John Thornley had a shoe repair shop just east of town. His sister Ellen from Pincher Creek was visiting him and was scheduled to take the train home the next day.

On a whim, John suggested they stay the night at the hotel in Frank as it was closer to the station. She thought it was silly but agreed anyway; this chance decision saved their lives.

One of the most tragic stories is the fate of the William Warrington family. He survived because he was in the mine, but his wife and four children died in their home.

Part of the railway work crew that survived the Slide because they arrived in Frank a day late.

Twelve men living at a railway work camp in the middle of the Slide were all killed. But a crew of 128 others that was scheduled to join them the day before the Slide was saved. The new workers were in railway cars at a siding in Morrisey, B.C., waiting to be transported to Frank. The train that was to take them there forgot to pick them up as it went by, and that saved their lives.

John McVeigh, general manager of a construction crew camped east of Frank, normally returned to Blairmore each night where he and his wife and child stayed at a hotel. On the night of the Slide John's family was in Calgary visiting his wife's parents. He stayed over at the camp that night, and was killed along with the entire crew.

Robert Watt had been playing blackjack at the Imperial Hotel with his friend Les Ferguson. Les suggested that Robert stay over at the hotel with him, but his friend decided to return to his room above the livery stable. He never returned.

The Clarks with their two eldest children.

Mr. Clark was killed at the tipple, while his wife and five of their six children died in thier home. The eldest daughter, Lillian, on the right, worked at the boarding house and was persuaded to stay the night because she had worked a long day. She had never spent a night away from home in her life, but doing so saved her life, for the slide rock missed the boarding house.

Sightseers came from far and wide to see the Slide, many of them in special excursion trains.

How large was the Slide?

The mass of limestone that came down from Turtle Mountain was about 1,400 feet high, 3,000 feet wide, 500 feet thick, and weighed about 90 million tons. It covered about 1.2 square miles of the valley floor to an average depth of 45 feet, ranging in depth from 3 feet to 100 feet. The distance from the summit of the mountain to the end of the Slide, following the slope, is about 2.5 miles.

How many bodies were recovered from the Slide?

Only twelve bodies were recovered from the Slide. Six were members of the Leitch Family, and they were buried in Cranbrook B.C., where Mr. Leitch's brother lived. The other six were buried in Blairmore, because the Frank cemetery was covered by debris. Most of the victims were already buried deep within the Slide and few attempts were made to recover them.

Was it the world's largest slide, or the most disastrous?

Frank Slide is very famous, but it is far from being the largest or the most destructive landslide in the world.

The most disastrous in terms of lost lives was at a mountain in Peru called Nevados Huascaran. The mountain has had two slides, in 1962 and 1970, that killed about 22,000 people, in total.

When Frank Slide occurred, there were no other landslides known in Canada that approached it in size. In 1965 the Hope Slide fell in B.C., covering an area one third greater than Frank and involving nearly twice as much rock, but it killed only five people. Frank has a much greater mystique than Hope, probably because it covered part of a town. Furthermore, the scar on the mountain and the outline of the slide rock at Frank are more spectacular, because their very light colour contrasts with the adjacent landscape.

In 1956, the prehistoric Downie Slide was discovered in the upper Columbia River Valley of British Columbia. About 2,750 million tons of rock slid, making it one of the largest in the world, and about 30 times as large as Frank. Downie occurred about 10,000 years ago, long before recorded history, and now the forest has grown over it.

Is there ANY buried treasure under the Slide?

Sam Ennis related that the day before the Slide an Italian was called to Macleod to give evidence at a trial. When the man returned to Frank, a pile of rocks lay where his shack had stood. He frantically searched the place, looking for the 'big fir tree.' His life savings of $700.00 was buried at the foot of it. He never found the fir tree or the money, but he was alive, and was luckier than his neighbours.

Sid Choquette saves the Passenger Train.

A CPR freight train barely escaped the Slide, because the crew had heard the falling rock mass and drove westward to safety. Arriving at the Frank Station, they learned that a passenger train was east of the Slide and heading toward it. The telegraph line was down so the train could not be warned.

With incredible daring the brakeman, Sid Choquette, set out to walk across the Slide to warn the oncoming train. Somehow he managed to scramble across the unstable pile of rock, not knowing how wide it was, yet groping through the dust and keeping on course for over a mile. He made it, stumbling off the eastern side with incredible accuracy, just in time to flag down the Passenger Train as it rolled through the darkness. The CPR presented Sid with a cheque for $25.00, and a letter of commendation.

Rock covering the rail line after Frank Slide, a scene that would greet the Passenger Train.

The Passenger Train, saved from danger, flagged down by Sid Choquette as it steamed toward Frank after the Slide.

What happened to the railway lines?

There were three railway lines in Frank, and all were partly covered by the Slide (page 11). The Crowsnest branch of the CPR was a main transcontinental line and it was covered for 7,000 feet. Two spur lines joined the main line at Frank. A short one picked up coal cars at the mine, and the part of it near the mine entrance was covered. A longer spur line, the Frank and Grassy Mountain Railway, was being completed by a twelve man construction crew camped east of town. It was intended to bring coal from Lille, a town north of Frank. That spur was covered for about 5,000 feet.

The CPR ran a makeshift service through the Pass until its rail line was rebuilt. Trains came to the Slide from both sides, and the passengers and mail were shunted around by stage coach on a newly constructed wagon trail. On the other side the journey was resumed by rail.

A large construction crew was on the way to Frank when the Slide occurred, so it went right to work on the CPR line. With manpower, teams of horses and dynamite they rebuilt the line, and trains were using it three weeks after the Slide. The new cut followed the old one, with the new tracks laid down at a higher level. It was very important to get the railway operating again quickly, because it was the lifeline of the Pass and a main route across Canada.

Rebuilding the CPR line across Frank Slide, 1903.

Steam engine on the Frank and Grassy Mountain line in 1906, rebuilt after the Slide. Fireman Alb May and engineer Jack Williams are on the catwalk.

The Slide made a useful quarry

After their tracks were rebuilt, the Canadian Pacific Railway began to haul slide rock to other parts of Western Canada to be used for fill and retaining walls. A steamshovel was stationed permanently on a siding in the Slide and it loaded rock onto flatcars.

The CPR continued to haul slide rock for many years after the railway was rebuilt. This served to lower the bed and improve the grade, but they also widened the cut greatly, simply to obtain more rock. The Slide became a valuable quarry for the CPR.

What happened to the road?

The road through Frank at the time of the Slide was just a wagon trail, as there were no motorized vehicles in the Pass. When the road was covered by slide rock, a new one was quickly built around the north border of the Slide.

Building a new road across the Slide was a much bigger job. It took nearly three years, and the road was not opened until April 14, 1906.

Carriage on first road built across the Slide. This was little more than a trail between the larger boulders, with occasional wider spots for passing.

The first automobile in the Pass. It was a Tudhope - McIntyre, and arrived in 1907 or '8. Cars honked before going around the big boulders in the Slide to warn oncoming vehicles of their presence.

Setting powder for the second road built over the Slide. It was built in the early 1930's during the Depression, and was partly a make work project.

Roads in the Slide are an engineer's delight. They are difficult to build, but easy to maintain. The base of broken rock has excellent drainage, no compaction problems, and no frost heaving.

Vacating the town after the Slide

Frank Slide was a major disaster, so Premier Haultain went there immediately to take charge. On May 2nd he learned that there were fissures at the top of the mountain that had not been there before the Slide. Fearing another slide, he called a public meeting that night and told the people to leave, adding that if they did not he would have them removed.

The CPR provided two trains of box cars, and soon after they arrived nearly everyone was on board with their household goods, ready to move. Soon the town was deserted, except for a police guard.

The geologists decide that it is safe to return to town

The Geological Survey of Canada (GSC) sent two of its most respected geologists to Frank within days of the Slide, R.G. McConnell and R.W. Brock. They agreed to report by May 11 on whether it was safe to return to the town.

R.G. McConnell

When the peak of Turtle Mountain fell away, two new peaks were created on the sides, and they were soon named North Peak and South Peak. North Peak was regarded as the most dangerous, because

R.W. Brock

it was right abovethe town and very steep. It was, however, supported by a strong shoulder on the east, so the geologists felt the town was not in immediate danger. Word was sent out that people could return to Frank, and they flocked back.

Frank recovered from its tragedy with incredible speed. In 1904 Inspector Davidson of the NWMP reported that Frank had completely recovered, the population was about the same and business was brisk.

Starting a new townsite farther from North Peak

Construction resumed in the town of Frank right after the Slide, but it was at a new townsite just across the railway tracks. This was considered safer because it was not under North Peak.

An elegant house was built in 1906 for the Mine Manager, Mr. Gebo. The local kids called it 'The Castle.' It was still there in 1990, but the interesting roof and the top two floors had been re-moved, and modern siding was added.

The Gebo house at the new Frank townsite.

A geological commission studies the mountain

The GSC continued to monitor Turtle Mountain, and in 1910 Brock reported new fissures on the North Peak. He was very concerned about another slide, so the GSC set up a commission to study the mountain. Two eminent geologists and one mining engineer made the study.

The commission concluded that North Peak was very unstable and that continued mining would increase the danger. If the peak fell, it would cover all of the original townsite that had been missed by the 1903 slide. The commission recommended that the coal com-pany use more cautious mining methods. It also said that even without further mining the danger was great enough that all buildings in old Frank should be moved to the new townsite. Financial assistance was provided to those who wished to move.

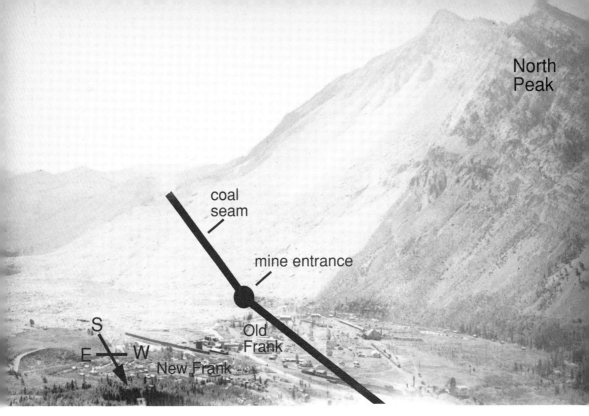

North Peak

coal
seam

mine entrance

S

E — W

Old
Frank

New Frank

View of Frank from the north in 1911. Geologists concluded that North Peak was unstable, and could slide onto old Frank.

After 1911, most of the buildings were moved from old Frank to new Frank.

How long did the town exist after the Slide?

Many of the people living in Frank at the time of the Slide returned, because people are naturally optimistic. When the mine resumed production and then increased it, new people arrived as well. As long as the mine flourished they remained and the population of the town grew.

Sadly, the mining industry in the Crownsest Pass has had a turbulent history of booms and busts. There were strikes, explosions, fires, and shutdowns because of poor markets. Through all these events, the fate of the town was tied directly to that of the mine.

After a long history of problems, the Frank Mine finally closed for good in 1918. From then on the town quickly declined, many of the merchants and workers moving to Blairmore. There was still a settlement at Frank in 1990, but with a smaller population. The 1903 slide does not seem to influence whether or not people remain in Frank.

What happened to the coal mine?

Many assume that after the Slide the mine at Frank closed permanently, but this was not the case. The owners were very anxious to resume production, and the mine was operating again in about a month. Soon the tracks, tipple and plant were rebuilt and the mine was back to full production. Then a second mine was begun north of the town, and by 1910 the company was producing far more coal than it had before the Slide.

Re-opening the mine at Frank by removing rock that filled the entrance.

The rebuilt mine entrance at Frank after the Slide.

The new tipple at Frank, built after the Slide. It is at the site of the former tipple, well within the slide area.

There has been great debate about whether mining coal at Frank was one of the causes of the Slide. Government geologists said that it was, and that more mining could cause another. The mine owners and their consultants maintained that the mine did not in any way cause the Slide. The truth will never be known.

Within a few days of the Slide the Canadian American Coal and Coke Company made a decision to re-open the mine. Their consulting engineer, Mr. Dowlen wrote that "...the mining operations at Frank bear no relation whatever to the rock slide."

In the years after the Slide the coal mining industry had problems, and these affected Frank as well as other operators in the Pass. There were mining disasters, strikes, and market collapses. But Frank had an additional problem - removing coal might cause another slide. Very stringent mining practises had been recommended by the Geological Commission.

The Frank mine closed in 1918 and has never re-opened. There were many reasons, for closing, a combination of all their problems. The last straw however was a disastrous underground fire in the mine.

What happened to Crowsnest River?

Crowsnest River was dammed by the Slide and backed up to form Frank Lake.

When the Slide dammed Crowsnest River, the rising water flooded the lower tunnel of the mine. For a few days there was fear that the water might also back up and flood the town of Frank. These fears were soon dispelled when a surveyor took levels and determined that the water would spill over the slide rock long before it flooded the town. That soon happened and the river resumed its flow eastward to the prairies.

Chaining the mountain

In the 1930's markers were put on either side of the fissures in Turtle Mountain, and the distance between them was measured periodically. The object was to check for any movement. This was referred to as 'chaining,' because the measuring was done with a long steel measuring tape called a chain.

A tourist stopping for gas at a local service station asked the attendant if he was afraid to live and work so near this mountain.

"Oh, no," replied the attendant. "They have just been up and re-chained it."

What did the public think caused the Slide?

Frank Slide received tremendous newspaper coverage around the world. The press reported many opinions on its cause, including an earthquake, a volcano, an explosion of coal gas in the mine, and a meteorite striking the mountain.

The Frank Sentinel reported that there must have been an explosion of gas that had been accumulating in a big cave or crevice near the top of Turtle Mountain. It was believed that coal gas had leaked up from the mine to the cave, where it combined with lime and water to make an explosive mixture.

Mr. William Pearce, a mine inspector, arrived in Frank soon after the disaster and said that everyone in Frank believed a volcano had caused the Slide. One of the things that convinced them was that 'fire' was observed at the time.

The so-called fire may be explained by the presence of chert (flint) in the limestone slide rock. As the rocks slid over one another, the friction produced sparks which the locals called 'fire.' There could also have been visible electrical discharges created by the cloud of dust.

The Air Cushion Theory

The debris from Frank Slide travelled much farther than we calculate it should have. Larger slides travel even farther. Clearly, some unknown process affects slides over a certain size, so that the bigger they are the farther they go. This process makes a large mass of broken dry rocks flow like a liquid.

One explanation, the air cushion theory, suggests that the rock mass rides upon a layer of compressed air trapped beneath it. Another is that the rock is lubricated by dust or air. Still another is that the mass has an acoustic or seismic energy - a shaking - that vibrates the whole mass and reduces the friction.

What did the experts think caused the Slide?

Geologists McConnell and Brock did a detailed study of Turtle Mountain, the Slide, and the Frank Mine right after the disaster. They said the Slide was due to a combination of causes.

The primary cause was the form and structure of Turtle Mountain - it had a hard, unstable limestone ledge at the top. The instability was due in part to the fact that the face of the limestone was a steep cliff. This steepness was caused by selective erosion. The base of the mountain was softer rock that was easily eroded away by the river and former glaciers. The limestone, on the other hand, was hard, and resisted erosion, so became steeper and steeper as time passed.

Removing coal from large chambers in the mine at the base of the mountain, would also have contributed to the instability by allowing collapse of the rock above the coal seam. Earthquakes not long before the Slide might have weakened the rocks as well.

The final trigger may have been the weather. For a few days before the Slide it was very hot, and meltwater may have entered fissures in the top of the mountain.

On the night of the Slide it was very cold, down to Zero (^{0}F), which may have frozen water in the fissures and expanded them. This could tip the balance and allow the unstable mass to finally break away.

The conclusions of McConnell and Brock in 1903 are still regarded as sound and all the factors they listed are still considered to have contributed to the Slide. As scientists, however, we do not completely agree on which factors were the most important. It is widely accepted that the structure of the mountain was the main factor, and that the influence of weather was very minor. The main disagreement concerns the role of mining.

Brock was quite confident that opening chambers in the mine was an important cause of the Slide. In 1910 he wrote that "Of the various causes which were responsible for the big slide there can be no question but that the mining of coal was a prime one."

The part of the peak that fell was precisely up slope from the part of the coal seam that had been mined (page 10). This supports the suggestion that mining was a factor in causing the Slide.

How Turtle Mountain formed

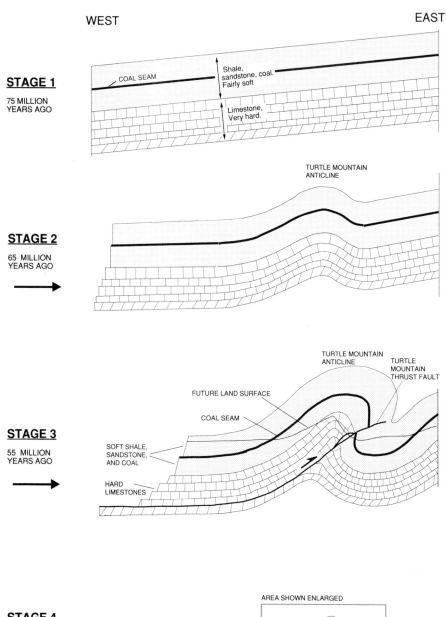

WEST

EAST

STAGE 1

75 MILLION
YEARS AGO

COAL SEAM

Shale,
sandstone, coal.
Fairly soft

Limestone,
Very hard.

STAGE 2

65 MILLION
YEARS AGO

TURTLE MOUNTAIN
ANTICLINE

STAGE 3

55 MILLION
YEARS AGO

TURTLE MOUNTAIN
ANTICLINE

TURTLE
MOUNTAIN
THRUST FAULT

FUTURE LAND SURFACE

COAL SEAM

SOFT SHALE,
SANDSTONE,
AND COAL

HARD
LIMESTONES

STAGE 4

APRIL 1903,
BEFORE THE
SLIDE

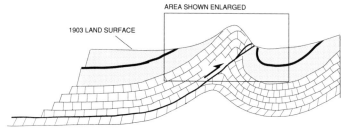

AREA SHOWN ENLARGED

1903 LAND SURFACE

Turtle Mountain took millions of years to form, but there were only four important stages. They are shown on the opposite page.

Stage 1. A layer of sedimentary rocks more than six miles thick covered Western Canada, dipping gently to the west. The lower part was mainly limestone, hard by nature, but hardened further because it was buried deeply and under great pressure. The upper part of the layer was shale, sandstone, and thin coal seams. These are naturally softer rocks, but also were not hardened by deep burial.

Stage 2. Mountain building began, caused by forces that pushed the sedimentary layer eastward. At first, the beds were squeezed into gentle folds, one of them being the Turtle Mountain Anticline.

Stage 3. The pushing increased and the Turtle Mountain Thrust Fault developed under the anticline. The part of the layer above the fault separated from more rigid rocks beneath, and slid eastward on the fault surface. This sliding intensified and faulted the Turtle Mountain Anticline. At the end of Stage 3 deformation stopped, so the shapes of the structures did not change after that. The shape of the land surface changed greatly however, because erosion continued until Stage 4, and continues today as well.

Stage 4. This cross section represents Turtle Mountain in 1903, just before the Slide. The land surface developed after mountain building had stopped, and resulted from river and glacial erosion of the Stage 3 cross section. The rocks and formations in the two lower cross sections have exactly the same shapes. Everything above the line marked Future Land Surface in Stage 3 was simply stripped off by erosion to produce the 1903 land surface shown in Stage 4.

The setting of Turtle Mountain shown by Stage 4 is enlarged at the top of page 44.

Why the Slide occurred

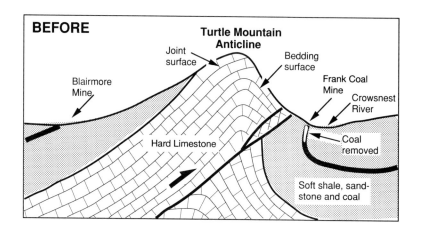

BEFORE

Turtle Mountain
Anticline

Joint surface

Bedding surface

Blairmore Mine

Frank Coal Mine

Crowsnest River

Coal removed

Hard Limestone

Soft shale, sand-stone and coal

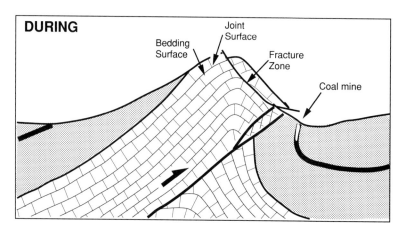

DURING

Joint Surface

Bedding Surface

Fracture Zone

Coal mine

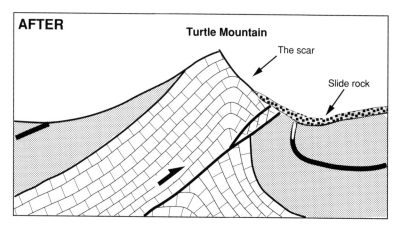

AFTER

Turtle Mountain

The scar

Slide rock

Over millions of years, nature had created a situation on Turtle Mountain that made a slide inevitable, but some action triggered the event at a precise moment in 1903. We have a good idea of what triggered the Slide, and this is summarized on the opposite page.

Before the Slide. Turtle Mountain is part of an anticline, so the beds dipped west on the west side, curved over the top, and dipped east on the east side. The limestone in the peak, like most limestone, was riddled by flat planes of weakness cutting through it - bedding surfaces and joint surfaces.

Bedding surfaces are between beds, the sedimentary layers that formed when the rock was deposited. Bedding in rock is like the grain in wood. Layers of different composition formed one after the other, and they created long zones of weakness and easy splitting. Limestone can be pulled apart or slid apart along bedding surfaces with relative ease.

Joint surfaces are shorter cracks in the rock, and most of them cut across the beds at right angles. Joints do not continue for long distances as beds do, but they still provide a second direction of weakness, because they are so numerous and tend to be aligned.

There was a long, steep, east dipping zone of weakness in Turtle Mountain. It was there by co-incidence because it had two shorter parts that were lined up end to end. The lower part of the zone followed beds near the base of the mountain, and the upper part followed joints near the top. Nothing would have happened to this zone if it were not for another unusual coincidence - the peak was poorly supported.

During the Slide. Removal of coal at the base of Turtle Mountain allowed the rocks west of the seam to collapse slightly to the east. This allowed the ledge above to tip slightly to the east and become steeper. On the night of the Slide, water freezing and expanding in the limestone fissures shifted the ledge a tiny bit farther east again. At last a portion of the mountain became too great for the base to support, and gravity took over to break it free. The zone of weakness became a fracture zone, and the rock above it plummeted into the valley below.

It took millions of years to set the stage, but the event was over in seconds.

Is Turtle Mountain still moving?

The Turtle Mountain Study Group of Alberta Environment monitored the mountain to determine if another slide was about to occur, and to give advance warning.

The group studied fissures to see if there is movement on them. Special sensors are mounted within them to detect movement. Markers

Strain gauges placed within a fissure to determine if the sides are moving apart. The cover has been removed from the upper sensor.

are set on either side of fissures to measure if the sides are moving apart. The observations so far show that there has been little movement.

The group also monitors seismic activity with modern equipment. Local earth tremors (earthquakes) do occur within Turtle Mountain. They are extremely small and probably result from minor settling of the mountain due to continued collapse of the coal mine beneath its southeast flank.

The study group believes that it would detect signs of a future slide well in advance, and that warnings could be issued. Major slides do not just suddenly occur, but show signs of impending failure by an acceleration of movement or deformation over a period of time. There is evidence that there were events before the 1903 slide that could have foretold it if they had been properly interpreted. The miners had noticed excessive slumping of coal from the walls. They had also noticed rumblings that were more extreme and that were deeper within the mountain than they had experienced in other mines. Presumably these were adjustments within the mountain that occurred because of the mining.

Could there be another slide at Frank?

There has been endless speculation on this question, and the real answer is "no one knows." When the peak in the central part of Turtle Mountain fell in 1903, it became a low area, and that part of the mountain probably will not fall again.

When the peak fell two new peaks were created to the north and south. North Peak overhangs the town, and for some years it was regarded as the least stable, because it has the steepest eastern face. Present opinion is that South Peak is the least stable because it is not supported well. A new industrial park is located at the site of the old town of Frank, and would be endangered if North Peak were to fall.

Most geologists agree that there could be another slide at Frank if enough time is allowed, because the erosion that produced the instability is still going on. We can't agree on how much rock might fall though, or how far the debris would travel. We also don't know whether it will happen next year or 10,000 years from now.

What's in the future for Frank Slide?

The slide rock and the scar have been there for several generations. They will be there for many more, but they will not be there forever. Nature is taking care of that.

Trees are already beginning to creep in from the margins and grow over the Slide. The rocks are not quite as white and fresh as they were in early photographs. They are being weathered by the elements and are slowly eroding. Wind blown dust that settles on the rock washes into the low spots and gives plants a better place to grow. Their roots, in an endless search for nutrients, then widen any cracks they find, break the rocks up a little more, and gradually turn it to soil.

It has been suggested that the trees be cut down so the Slide will remain visible forever. This is not allowed, because the Slide is officially an historic site, and cannot be tampered with. The attempt would eventually fail anyway. Nature is slowly correcting her mistake, and she will outlast us all.

Frank Slide Interpretive Centre, built in 1986, is operated year round by the Department of Culture and Community Spirit of the Government of Alberta. It provides a good history of the Slide and of the Crowsnest Pass.

Do the local people fear another landslide?

The people of Frank and other parts of the Pass rarely think about whether Turtle Mountain will fall again. They do not let the potential danger influence their lives. Instead they regard the Slide as a fascinating site to see, to climb over and to live beside. They know its history but they don't look back and dwell on tragedy.